Exploring the DOMINICAN REPUBLIC

with the FIVE Themes of Geography

by Amy Marcus

Rosen Classroom Books & Materials

Published in 2005 by The Rosen Publishing Group, Inc.
29 East 21st Street, New York, NY 10010

First Edition

Editor: Geeta Sobha
Book Design: Michelle Innes

Photo Credits: Cover, p. 1 © Ethel Davies/ImageState; pp. 9, 19, 21 (hills) © Tom Bean/Corbis; p. 9 (sugarcane) © Danny Lehman/Corbis; p. 9 (sugarcane field) © Marc Pokempner/Getty Images; p. 10 © Steven Hunt/Getty Images; p. 10 (iguana) © Giraud Philippe/Corbis Sygma; pp. 12, 19 (Santo Domingo) © Jeremy Horner/Corbis; p. 12 (woman) © Owen Franken/Corbis; pp. 12 (bohios), 15 © Richard Bickel/Corbis; p. 15 (coffee beans) © Dag Sunberg/Getty Images; p. 16 © AP/Wide World Photos; p. 16 (bridge) © Adam Woolfitt/Corbis; p. 19 (newspaper) © Tony Arruza/Corbis; p. 21 (La Romana) © Jonathan Morgan/Getty Images

Library of Congress Cataloging-in-Publication Data

Marcus, Amy.
    Exploring the Dominican Republic with the five themes of geography / by Amy Marcus.— 1st ed.
        p. cm. — (The library of the Western Hemisphere)
    Summary: Briefly looks at the Dominican Republic's geography in terms of five geographical themes: location; place, or physical characteristics; human-environment interaction; movement, or transportation; and region.
    ISBN 1-4042-2671-0 (lib. bdg.) — ISBN 0-8239-4631-2 (pbk.)
    1. Dominican Republic—Geography—Juvenile literature. [1. Dominican Republic—Geography.] I. Title. II. Series.

    F1935.5.M37 2005
    917.293—dc22

                                                              2003022248

Manufactured in the United States of America

Contents

The FIVE Themes of Geography

Geography is the study of Earth, including its physical features, resources, climate, and people. To study a particular country or area, such as the Dominican Republic, we use the five themes of geography: location, place, human-environment interaction, movement, and regions. We use these five themes to organize and understand important information about the geography of our world, including the Dominican Republic.

1 Location

Where is the Dominican Republic?

We can define where the Dominican Republic is by using its absolute, or exact, location. Absolute location tells exactly where a place is in the world. We use the imaginary lines of longitude and latitude to show the absolute location of a place.

You can also use the Dominican Republic's relative, or general, location to define where it is. Relative location describes where a place is in relation to other places near it. The cardinal directions of east, west, north, and south are also used to define the relative location of a place.

2 Place

What is the Dominican Republic like?

To answer this question, we must study the physical and human features of the Dominican Republic. The physical features include landforms, natural resources, bodies of water, climate, and plant and animal life. The human features are things, such as cities, buildings, government, and traditions, that have been created by people.

3 Human-Environment Interaction

How do the people and the environment of the Dominican Republic affect each other?

Human-environment interaction explains how the environment of the Dominican Republic has affected the way its people live. It also explains how the people have adapted to the environment, or how they have changed it.

4 Movement

How do people, goods, and ideas get from place to place in the Dominican Republic?

This theme explains how products, people, and ideas move around within the Dominican Republic. It also shows how they move from the Dominican Republic to other parts of the world.

5 Regions

What does the Dominican Republic have in common with other places? How are places within the Dominican Republic grouped?

A region is made up of different places that are grouped together because they share a common feature. This theme studies the physical and cultural features that the Dominican Republic shares with other areas. It also explores regions within the Dominican Republic.

The absolute location of the Dominican Republic is 19° north and 70° west.

You can find the Dominican Republic's relative location by looking at the places that surround it. On the western border of the Dominican Republic is the country of Haiti. The Dominican Republic is bordered on the north by the Atlantic Ocean and on the south by the Caribbean Sea.

Where in the World?

Absolute location is the point where the lines of longitude and latitude meet.

Longitude tells a place's position in degrees east or west of the prime meridian, a line that runs through Greenwich, London.

Latitude tells a place's position in degrees north or south of the equator, the imaginary line that goes around the middle of the earth.

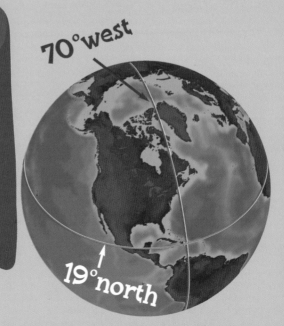

70° west

19° north

The Dominican Republic is located on the island of Hispaniola, one of the islands in the West Indies. The capital city is Santo Domingo.

Bahamas

Atlantic Ocean

Cuba

Hispaniola

Cordillera Oriental

Haiti

Dominican Republic

Santo Domingo

Caribbean Sea

N
W E
S

Physical Features

Most of the Dominican Republic's land is made up of mountains. This is because Hispaniola is actually created from the peaks of underwater mountains. Duarte Peak is the highest mountain in the Dominican Republic. It reaches 10,417 feet (3,175 meters) and is located in the Cordillera Central mountain range.

The Cibao Valley is the country's most fertile area, where most crops are grown. It lies between the Cordillera Central and a smaller mountain range, the Cordillera Septentrional. The Cordillera Septentrional is the mountain range in the northern part of the country.

Rivers in the Dominican Republic include the Yaque del Sur in the southwest and the Yaque del Norte in the northwest. The largest natural lake is Lake Enriquillo, which is the lowest point in the West Indies.

Sugarcane is grown in the eastern part of the Dominican Republic, where the land is less mountainous.

Pico Duarte is the highest mountain in the West Indies.

The rhinoceros iguana can only be found on the island of Hispaniola, in both Haiti and the Dominican Republic.

Green sea turtles are one of four types of turtles found in the coastal waters of the Dominican Republic.

The Dominican Republic has a warm, tropical climate throughout the year. The temperature ranges between 60°F (16°C) and 90°F (32°C). For most of the country, the rainy season lasts from May through November. The Dominican Republic is often threatened by dangerous hurricanes.

Among the animals found in the Dominican Republic are alligators, iguanas, turtles, waterfowl, and agoutis, a type of rodent. The national bird is the cigua palmera. The Ridgway's hawk and the ashy face owl are only found on Hispaniola.

Many beautiful trees can be found in the Dominican Republic, including mahogany, rosewood, and cacao, from which chocolate is made.

These are the homes of farmworkers in Valle Nuevo. The houses are called *bohios.*

Cacao is a principal crop in the Dominican Republic. The cacao bean is used to make cocoa and chocolate.

The Cathedral Santa Maria la Menor was the first cathedral built in the Western Hemisphere.

Human Features

Over 8,700,000 people live in the Dominican Republic. The people are mostly mulatto, meaning that they are descended from both European and African peoples. More than half of the people live in urban areas. The rest live in rural farmlands. About half of the people are farmers. Many Dominicans work in processing sugar-cane, coffee, and cacao bean. Others work in mining of natural resources such as nickel, gold, and limestone.

The culture has strong Spanish and African influences. Spanish is the official language of the Dominican Republic. Dominican music has strong Latin and African rhythms. It can be clearly heard in their most popular form of music and dance, merengue.

The people of the Dominican Republic depend on the country's wealth of natural resources. During heavy rainfalls, water flows down from the mountains, bringing soil filled with nutrients to the valleys. Dominicans grow fruits, vegetables, rice, sugarcane, and tobacco in the valleys of the Yuna, Yaque del Norte, San Juan, and Yaque del Sur rivers. They also grow coffee plants and cacao in lower mountain regions.

Most of the people in the Dominican Republic work in areas related to the country's natural resources. Because the Dominican Republic is an island, the ocean is important for Dominicans. Many people make their living by fishing, and fish is an important part of their diets, especially along the coastal areas. They also make salt from sea water. Also, salt is mined from rock deposits near Lake Enriquillo.

Until the 1980s, agriculture was an important part of the Dominican Republic's economy. Today, mining, manufacturing, and tourism are the most important parts of the country's economy.

These fishermen are from Bayahibe, a coastal fishing village in the southeast of the Dominican Republic. The town is also a well-known tourist area.

Santo Domingo is the financial and industrial center of the Dominican Republic. Plastic, cement, and food processing are among its important industries.

Many Dominicans see the effects of mining gold as harmful to the environment.

The main ways that people have changed the environment of the Dominican Republic are through urbanization, or building cities, and by mining. Mining of gold, silver, iron ore, and aluminum ore has become important to business in the Dominican Republic. Also, the people have created large sugarcane plantations, which are found in the southeastern part of the country.

Cities have replaced many small villages, primarily along the southern coast. With cities, usually come factories and pollution. At this time, however, pollution has not been a serious problem.

The major negative effect of human activity has been the reduction of forest areas due to the cutting down of trees. However, the government regulates the amount of trees that are cut.

4 Movement

The Dominican Republic's transportation center is its capital, Santo Domingo. From there, people and goods can reach all parts of the country.

Most of the roads in the Dominican Republic are not paved, and few Dominicans have cars. To get from place to place, they travel in buses, vans, and trucks. In rural areas, the people may live quite far from decent roads. Often, they travel by foot or on horseback.

Most goods are transported around the country by truck or by train. The train system in the Dominican Republic is mainly used for moving goods, not people. To move goods out of or into the country, there are several ports that allow shipping.

The Dominican Republic has 10 major newspapers. It also has well over 100 radio stations and about 25 television stations.

5 Regions

The Dominican Republic is part of a geographical region known as the West Indies. The West Indies is a group of islands that stretches from south of Florida to the northern coast of South America.

Natural regions within the Dominican Republic include the Atlantic coastal plain and the Cordillera Septentrional in the north. There is also the Sierra de Neiba and Sierra de Baoruco in the southwest.

The Dominican Republic is considered part of Latin America. Latin America is made up of countries where most people speak a Romance language, such as Spanish, French, or Portuguese. These countries are located south of the United States.

Politically, the Dominican Republic is broken into 29 provinces and one national district, Santo Domingo.

The Yaque del Norte is the largest river in the Dominican Republic.

Atlantic Ocean

La Romana, in the southeast of the Dominican Republic, is a destination for many tourists from all over the world.

Cordillera Septentrional

Cibao Valley

Cordillera Central

Sierra de Neiba

Yaque del Sur

Rio Ozama

Sierra de Baoruco

The waters of the *Yaque del Sur* are used to grow rice, sugarcane, beans, bananas, and peanuts.

Caribbean Sea

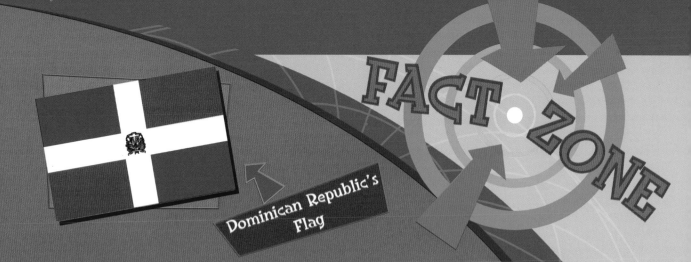

Dominican Republic's Flag

FACT ZONE

Population (2003) 8,715,602

Language Spanish

Absolute location 19°north, 70°west

Capital city Santo Domingo

Area 18,816 square miles (4,734 square kilometers)

Highest point Pico Duarte 10,417 feet (3,175 meters)

Lowest point Lake Enriquillo -151 feet (-46 m)

Land boundaries Haiti

Natural resources Gold, nickel, silver, tin, marble, limestone

Agricultural products avocados, coffee, mangoes, rice, sugarcane, tobacco, cocoa beans

Major exports sugar and sugar products, nickel, gold, coffee, cocoa, and tobacco

Major imports machinery, iron, steel, petroleum and petroleum products, and chemicals

Glossary

cacao (kuh-KAW) A tree that produces a seed from which cocoa and chocolate are made.

culture (KUHL-chur) The way of life, ideas, customs, and traditions shared by a group of people.

descended (di-SEND-ud) To belong to a later generation of the same family.

interaction (in-tur-AK-shuhn) The action between people, groups, or things.

processing (PROSS-ess-ing) Preparing or changing by a series of steps.

province (PROV-uhnss) A district or region of some countries.

region (REE-juhn) An area or a district.

republic (ri-PUHB-lik) A form of government in which the people have the power to elect representatives who manage the government.

resource (ri-SORSS) Something that is valuable or useful to a place or person.

rural (RUR-uhl) Having to do with the countryside or farming.

tropical (TROP-uh-kuhl) To do with the hot, rainy area of the tropics.

urban (UR-buhn) Having to do with or living in a city.

Index

Web Sites

Due to the changing nature of Internet links, PowerKids Press has developed an on-line list of Web sites related to the subject of this book. This site is updated regularly. Please use this link to access the list:
http://www.powerkidslinks.com/lwh/domrep